The Last Decade

Poems by

Norman Rosten

Selected Works By the Author

POETRY
Return Again, Traveler. Yale University Press, 1940
The Fourth Decade and Other Poems. Farrar & Rinehart, Inc., 1943
Seven Poets In Search of an Answer: A Poetic Symposium. Bernard Ackerman, Inc., 1944
   (Maxwell Bodenheim, Joy Davidman, Langston Hughes, Aaron
     Kramer, Alfred Kreymborg, Martha Millet, Norman Rosten.)
The Big Road, A Narrative Poem. Rinehart & Co., Inc., 1946
Songs For Patricia. Illustrated by Alexander Dobkin, Simon and Schuster, 1951.
The Plane and the Shadow. Bookman Associates, 1953
Thrive Upon the Rock, New Poems. Trident Press, 1965
Selected Poems. George Braziller, 1979

RECORDING
The Poems of Norman Rosten. Folkways Records, 1963

NOVELS
Under the Boardwalk. Prentice-Hall, 1968; University of Arkansas Press, 1991
Over and Out. George Braziller, 1972
Love in All Its Disguises. Arbor House. 1981
Neighborhood Tales. George Braziller. 1986

CHILDREN'S BOOKS
The Wineglass: A Passover Story. Illustrated by Kaethe Zemach, Walker and Co., 1978
A City Is. Illustrated by Melanie Hope Greenberg, Edited by Patricia Rosten Filan,
   Henry Holt & Co., 2004

NONFICTION
Marilyn: An Untold Story. Signet Books, 1973; later published as *Marilyn: A Very Personal
   Story.* Millington, Ltd., 1974
Marilyn Among Friends. Sam Shaw and Norman Rosten, Bloomsbury, 1987; Henry Holt
   & Co., 1988

PLAYS
This Proud Pilgrimage. 1938 (University of Michigan); 1940 (Heckscher Theatre, NYC)
First Stop To Heaven. 1941 (Winsor Theatre, NYC)
Mardi Gras. 1954, Music by Duke Ellington (Walnut Street Theatre, Philadelphia, PA)
Mister Johnson. 1956 (Martin Beck Theatre, NYC), 1960 (Lyric Opera House, London)
The Golden Door. 1966 (HB Playwrights Foundation, NYC)
Come Slowly, Eden: A Portrait of Emily Dickenson. 1966 (Theatre De Lys, NYC)

OPERA
Shadows Among Us. Opera in II Acts, by Ezra Laderman, libretto by Norman Rosten, 1967
Worship. Opera in One Act by Ezra Laderman, libretto by Norman Rosten, 1974
The Marquesa of O. Opera in III Acts by Elie Sigmeister, libretto by Norman Rosten, 1982
Marilyn. Opera in II Acts, by Ezra Laderman, libretto by Norman Rosten, 1993

SCREENPLAYS
Land of White Alice. Directed by Willard Van Dyke, 1959
A View From the Bridge. Based on play by Arthur Miller. Directed by Sidney Lumet, 1962

The Last Decade

© 1992 by Norman Rosten
Edited by Ronald Thomas Rollet
Introduction © 2016 by Ronald Thomas Rollet
This Edition © 2016 Estate of Norman Rosten
and Patricia Rosten Filan
Cover photo of Brooklyn Bridge © 1959 Henrik Krogius

First Edition

ISBN 978-0-9895609-7-9
Library of Congress Control Number: 2016960014

All rights reserved. No part of this book may be reproduced or transmitted in any form or by any means, electronic or mechanical, including photocopying, recording or by any information storage or retrieval system without written permission from the author, except for inclusions of brief quotations in a review.

Printed in the United States of America
Cover and interior pages designed by SeaGrove Press

SeaGrove Press
638 Sunset Blvd
Cape May, New Jersey 08204
seagrovepress@gmail.com

For Patricia

Acknowledgements

The following poems were previously published:

"Matisse and the Dove" in *The New York Quarterly*, Number 1, Winter 1970.
"Weight" in *The New York Quarterly*, Number 21, 1978.
"Brooklyn Bridge" in *West Hills Review*, Vol. 4, 1983-84.
"Pegasus On 10th Avenue," "Pocket Park" and "Belles Lettres" in *West Hills Review*, Vol. 5, 1985.
"The Meeting" and "Weight: Brooklyn Bridge" in *The Niagra Magazine*, No. 12-13, Fall 1980.
"Lexington Avenue" in *Pivot*, No. 34, 1984.
"Houses" and "The Dead Think Only of Their Bodies" in *Pivot*, No. 38, 1990.
"Short Poem On the Long View" in *Hika*, Vol. xxviii, No. 3, Spring-Summer 1966.
"Baby Whale In Captivity" in *The Dolphin's Arc*, SCOP Publications, Inc., 1989.
"The Meeting," "The Dead Think Only of Their Bodies," "Poetry Day at the Whitehouse," "The Rings of Saturn," "Spring Spider," "Winter Birds," "Lexington Avenue," "Fifth Avenue," "Short Poem on the Long View," and "Handball Player" in *The Brooklyn College Alumni Literary Review*, Vol. 1, Nos. 1 and 2, Spring-Summer 1981.

Contents

Introduction	iv
I. Moving	1
Houses	2
The Fifth Year	3
The Tree And The Brook	4
Short Poem On The Long View	5
Views From Above	6
Interior	8
II. City/Cities	9
Brooklyn Bridge	10
Weight	12
Whitman Again	13
Brooklyn Handball Player	14
Grasshopper In Prospect Park	15
Music On The Brooklyn Barge	16
Poetry Day At The White House	17
Names	18
Apples In Leningrad	19
Fifth Avenue	21
Lexington Avenue	22
Prometheus Statue	23
Pocket Park—East Side	24
Pegasus On 10th Avenue	25
Wall Street	26
The Meeting	27
The River	28
III. Elegy (for Hedda)	29

IV. LOSSES & SILENCE	45
Losses	46
Silence	47
End Of The World	48
Triptych For Hedda	49
The Dead Think Only Of Their Bodies	52
Red	53
Alice Baber, Artist	54
Death Of A Magician	56
Music	57
Baby Whale In Captivity	58
V. THE TRANCE OF EROS	62
A. The Wound	62
B. Biography For Ipsithilla	84
VI. CREDO	97
Variations On A Willow Tree	98
Credo	99
Winter Birds	100
Spring Spider	101
Look Who's Here	102
The Canvas	103
Matisse And The Dove	104
On Eating The Lake Trout	105
The Rings Of Saturn	106
Belles Lettres	107
The Unfinished Poem	108
Consoling A Young Writer On A Rejection From A Literary Magazine	109
Aspects Of Ann	110
"More Poems! More Poems!"	115
Riddle	118
Finale	119
AUTHOR'S BIOGRAPHY	121

INTRODUCTION

The Last Decade is available to readers almost twenty-five years after Norman Rosten assembled these poems and asked if I could "re-organize [them] enough to get a book out of the material." That request began a year and a half of working together, editing this volume of collected poems.

It took no convincing for me to realize that *The Last Decade* is the culminating masterwork of this celebrated and gifted poet. The diversity in subject matter and style is a tribute to Norman Rosten's earned command of the poetic vocabulary.

Norman's first book of poetry, *Return Again Traveler*, won the prestigious Yale Series of Younger Poets award in 1940. Stephen Vincent Benét was the judge of the Yale Series at that time and turned down Norman's first submittal the previous year, although Benét included it in the final three manuscripts he shortlisted. In a letter to Norman, Benét proposed some changes and additions in orientation and topic. Instead of acting insulted at being told what to write or how to arrange his own material, Norman took all of these suggestions and resubmitted a very different text the following year.

That quality of ambition tempered by practical judgment characterized Norman Rosten's career as a writer—poet, playwright, novelist, biographer, librettist, journalist, children's book author and screenwriter. Norman was one of a select group of writers successful in practically every literary area and form. In addition to poetry, he wrote plays produced on Broadway and in London, fiction that received glowing front page reviews in the *New York Times Book Review*, best-selling non-fiction that told the story of his long friendship with Marilyn Monroe, award-winning screenplays and teleplays, librettos for operas performed at New York City Opera, a host of radio programs, as well as stories and articles published in a wide scope of literary journals, magazines, and newspapers.

However, Norman counted himsel a poet, first and last, publishing seven books of poetry as well as contributing to several more collections with other poets. "If," Norman confessed to me a year before he died, "I had my life as a writer to live again, I'd spend more time just writing poetry." He received many literary awards for his poetry in addition to the Yale Series of Younger Poets, including those from the American Academy of Arts and Letters and the Poetry Society of America. Norman won a Guggenheim Fellowship for poetry and was the recipient of the Ford Foundation Mentor Grant, matching him with a young poet receiving his first Foundation support (which is how I met Norman in 1965). Appropriately, Norman Rosten was chosen as the first Poet Laureate of Brooklyn, an honor recognizing him as the contemporary embodiment of that long line of Brooklyn poets (including five winners of the Pulitzer Prize in Poetry) that traces its lineage back to Walt Whitman.

In describing *The Last Decade*, Norman called the "Elegy: For Hedda" sequence, "the center of the poems." It is the emotional pivot point and contains his wrenching exploration of the intimate bonds that continue to link Norman and his wife, Hedda, after her death. "Elegy" documents his painful struggle to build a life again. The earthly fabric of their symbiotic relationship is torn apart and yet a new spiritual connection begins to form between them.

I found myself stunned by the "The Wound" and its visceral detailing of the affair between the older poet and his new lover. The knife-edge, carnal hunger exposed in these poems reveals a passion that I foolishly assumed was the territory of a younger man's love: sexual desire, jealousy, suspicion, envy, hatred, despair, longing, surrender, loss and the final acceptance

> *that love, once fled, consigns*
> *a man to a diminished life.*

"Elegy" and "The Wound" as well as the poems in the section *Losses & Silence* create powerful narrative tension around grief and erotic love and loss. The Quixotic sense of humor that informs "Biography of Ipsithilla" and poems such as "Short Poem On the Long View," in addition to many in the section *City/Cities*, represent contrasting and refreshing balancing acts of subject and composition by the poet.

Naturally enough for Brooklyn's Poet Laureate, *The Last Decade* contains many poems celebrating Brooklyn and especially its eponymous bridge. ("I take great comfort from the fact that I live around the corner from the most beautiful bridge in the world.") There are also poems that reflect the urbanness of Norman's spirit—such as "Brooklyn Handball Player" and "Grasshopper In Prospect Park."

His well-known love of Mozart and classical music (a theme found in many poems he published in his career and reflected in his opera librettos) is here delightfully recalled in "Music On the Brooklyn Barge." Bargemusic, a Brooklyn chamber music performance space that Norman tirelessly promoted, held a special memorial concert featuring selections from the many and varied musical compositions based on his poems.

One of the remarkable accomplishments of Norman Rosten as a writer was that he earned his income solely from writing. When a young and still unpublished Norman Mailer asked his Brooklyn Heights neighbor Norman Rosten how he was going to make a living if he didn't have a day job, Rosten said, "I intend to write one book with my right hand and another with my left." And he did.

Norman had an innate gift for friendship and a generous a heart. As proof, Mailer has written that it was Norman Rosten who took the typescript of *The Naked And The Dead* to his own publisher and convinced him to read and then publish Mailer's first novel—and the rest, as they say, is history. Mailer's "gift" from Norman Rosten was far from unique; Norman befriended with his counsel and publishing connections a long list of writers, myself included, and many owe the start or the continuation of their careers to his encouragement.

There is a kind of writer's karma involved for me in editing Norman's last book, since he was not only a mentor for almost three decades, but also the editor of my first book of poems. I initially argued against calling this collection *The Last Decade* because, as I said to Norman, that makes it sound like your final book and you will always have another one up your sleeve. Well, wherever good poets from Brooklyn go when they pass over, I'm sure Norman Rosten is still writing one book with his right hand and another with his left.

> The next life around, dear friends,
> let us study apples, and not stars.
>
> NORMAN ROSTEN
> *SHORT POEM ON THE LONG VIEW*

I. MOVING

Houses

Through a screen of trees, and a field beyond,
I hear the sharp hammer, the careful
spacing of nails into raw wood,
studs most likely. A good sound
to start the morning with.
                         A house
is under way, a one-man job
if I read the hammer right.

Each day, at my desk of wood,
that sound is a sweet hello.
I feel the kinship of our labors.
Weeks go by, trees for him
become 2x4's; for me, oxygen,
breath rather than possessions.
Yet, house enough for each.

Summer heat slows my work,
but not his steady rhythmic hammer.
I envy that precision.
                        By now
his roof is shingled, windows in,
doors about to be hung. Soon
the scaffolding will fall.
Days are short, the sun low,
and I'm still working on a wall.

The Fifth Year

My love had suffered the lower floor,
with death the last downward step;
I awoke, shuddered from my sleep
feeling released, but lost.

Five years to the month,
nothing's easier to assimilate
than time: I'm on a top floor,
a view assigned by Fate

who apparently has let me float
while love, like a kite's string,
keeps me swaying above the scene.
I feel her tugging fingers.

Higher to heaven, I try to sing,
but my song stays below,
that home I left, where we began
in hope and humorous poverty.

Years of dancing the lower floor!
She and I, once in our happiness,
now moon and shadow forever.
There are days I wish to jump.

The Tree and the Brook

He that's rooted,
she that flows by,
the reverse will do as well
for eternity.

The tree waits forever,
the brook can never return;
we can only waver
and keep warm.

To be rooted is a joy,
says the laughing tree;
while the water dances
on its way to the sea.

The doubting cloud
remains free,
floats with the wind
as you and me.

Short Poem on the Long View

As boys, we used to share a spyglass
that zoomed over rooftops to bring
a sunbathing girl against our eyes.
She drummed her fingers on a naked breast
and kept right on munching an apple.
We stared, we stared and sighed.

As men, we rushed into the breach of days,
forgetting rooftops in our lunge toward heaven.
In despair, we tried to pull the stars closer.
We consumed Utopia—or it consumed us:
The snake devouring its tail is the same snake
in a different composition. What wasted wars!

The next life around, dear friends,
let us study apples, and not stars.

VIEWS FROM ABOVE

Height, once my fear,
now reassures: I discover
close companions of the air—
blunt pigeon to lovely lark
test the currents, riding
easily from rooftop to ledge,
to glide by my window
for a look, then curving away.

Skyscrapers are defiant,
yet fade before the mist;
I watch them disappear
and emerge as though from
a photographic acid bath,
clear, sharp, emphatic.
At night, those high floors
become trays of diamonds;
lower, the lights flood upward
toward rooftop attic windows;
I'm a silent eavesdropper.
Weather washes over all,
color changing by the hour:
I have my own lily ponds,
born of Monet's music.

I who loved the movement of people
now find them too small
for interest; they're insects
reputed to be skillful with tools
but generally insignificant
to hurrying birds and copters
on various errands above the bridges.

The Last Decade

Sounds rise up, orchestral brass,
fire truck, ambulance, police truck
messengers sorting out
life, death, ordinary business.
We exist with elements of the day,
even as clouds return refreshed,
none of ours, sweeping over,
beauty above, given freely,
belonging to all.

INTERIOR

Sea mist on the boulders,
sea spray exploding with light:
it seems my own blood
has something of that play,
a desire of the elements
to join one another, seawater
clinging with salt to the rocks.

These are tides wrought
from the desperate acids of the world.
The shells grind in counterforce
along the seafloor: that turbulence
as deep within myself,
now pulled toward Asia,
now toward home.

II. CITY/CITIES

Brooklyn Bridge

It stands above a century of winds,
colossus anchored in tides,
still surprising the landscape.

Light upon the cables,
weight gathered within
the stone towers: a tension
spooled out as steel,
now compacted into giant shoulders.
On some days a lithograph,
on others a choir of strings,
our Gothic incarnation;
finally, a curve of silence
upholding a world, as Roebling dreamed …

The dream to reach beyond structure,
arrive at a waiting future:
and it is here.   Aloof to the age,
its beauty and line intact,
we see again the pink-veined stone
flowering to the arch, holding
the strands of cable woven by
forgotten fingers. The city flows
to the horizon, heavy with smoke
and the death of architecture,
yet the Bridge will soar, and sing,
rising with dawns and mists,
poised for another leap of time.

The Last Decade

Wheels accelerate on the span,
rasping like wasps in their madness,
drone of the living and the dead.
The century, begun on these cobbles,
turns on that weightless arc,
turns with the sun, with light,
as ghosts of the sailing ships
ride the same harbor.

WEIGHT

At dawn, when not observed,
empty of traffic, the bridge
groans and suffers
with its own weight.
The tension of those cables!
The equations of terror!
That arc across my dream
cracks my bones.
                    O God
(that other Weight), explain
if you will the agonized
balance of every object.
And hands, and kisses too,
are savored, saved (Sanctus!)
by this inherent power,
as love groans and suffers
with its own weight,
the weight of zero,
weight of stone.

WHITMAN AGAIN

Wind brings the moon over,
white ghost trailing his beard,
an astral emanation, once alien,
now a familiar visitor.

Rest awhile, Walt, at the Bridge.
We've learned to understand your power;
we're at ease with your universe,
its urgency and beatitude.

We've accepted your departure
and live with your precepts;
a peace toward all things,
of flesh, stone, and spirit.

Your lines are strands of the cables,
the singing arcs, our American music;
your voice the insistent aria
speaking of us, for us, our father.

Brooklyn Handball Player

His fate is hard and black,
a ricochet as fast
as light that splits the line
and gains the point.
                    The ball
is vengeance, his gloved hand
drives it to the corner
where it's curved, hangs
for a lucky out.
                    He waits
for a serve then fires
a bullet with a spinning
wrist that hugs the line
and skips to the left.
                    Point
is his, grips the ball,
skips it next to the right,
the wall responding,
and the city, hurrah,
that loves a Sunday winner!

Grasshopper in Prospect Park

Honey at my mouth, a frothing glue,
I give to you if properly coaxed:
O come for your honey, it's newly-
minted from under my green coat.

I lunge, I soar, I leap
from your fingers into the light,
without the slightest care
of how or where I navigate.

It doesn't matter: I'm spun of air,
I'm what's inside the bubble
with all my legs (I think they're six.)
The watching birds are all in a dazzle.

I rest, I doze, still on a stalk,
humming with the drone of summer;
honey at my mouth, born of my breath,
I dream beneath my green coat.

Music on the Brooklyn Barge

Noah had his Ark,
Olga her Barge; putting
the context aside, the cargo, the flood,
we think her Barge the truer miracle,
and made of superior wood.

Upon the tide of indifference
Olga's smile caught the wind,
and music came aboard: strings
and flutes and drums, paired or not,
just so they were hot.

The waters raged, the instruments
did not panic; Olga exclaimed,
"It's only the waves, not to worry;
play; if lost, we can't drift
very far; New Jersey or Staten,
batten down the scherzo,
cometh the dove, lovely adagio,
finale ahead, land, land!"

We made it. Applause, bravo,
and a new concert tomorrow!

Poetry Day at the White House

Poets arrive at the local Versailles,
searched for metaphors and explosives,
tagged and set free to wander.
Ahead, a reward of hors d'oeuvres;
the harmless punch freely flows.

Ambitions soon flare up,
dreams of grants and matching funds.
Astonishing poetesses, we bless
the carnal intrusion. Jealousies
(how did he/she get here?);
crew-cuts jostling the grayhairs,
young prosody verses old wisdom.
Under the chandeliers and portraits,
rumble of small thunder.

The President is out of town. His wife
shaking hands, a nightclub Queen.
Congressmen, con men, elbow-rubbers.
Readings and dealings all around.
There's Kunitz & Nims in tandem.
Where's Dickey & Ginsberg & Warren?
Who'll get the palm this year?
Let the wars go, the Muse is tame.
Not a single bloodstained line
to haunt the listeners.

In the bar car going back,
the anonymous night riding with us,
we few mix tea and bourbon,
somehow get to John Donne,
love sacred and profane;
his Elegies, our comforting world
against that city's ludicrous power.

NAMES
Vietnam Veterans Memorial
Washington, D.C.

As though it were actual speech,
a string of letters in an alphabet,
first seen at the edge of the grass,

the marble appearing alongside,
dipping with the earth's contour,
the letters lifted and flowed

into words (which are the names),
the black marble remorseless as history,
listing these deaths which glitter as stars

in the density of the firmament,
fading at daylight into names,
the reminding and hushed stone.

The air is quiet. Visitors stop, stare,
beyond speech and the vanished event,
and only the names calling out

to one another would know a language
to fit their death, which time has turned
into beauty, a crown for this place,

names who long for their departed bodies,
who long to speak but cannot,
who long to love but cannot.

Names at the farthest edge of the marble
meet the descending line of grass,
absorbed by the meadow, and the world.

APPLES IN LENINGRAD

Tired of morning art
and afternoon palaces
(Peter and Catherine and the royal lot),
I hungered for an apple;
an apple in Leningrad
would be a treat, a single apple
in whatever condition.

Since apples were always caviar
to my taste, at home or away,
their absence here was almost pain.
Nor did I have the word for apple
if one came my way. I cursed
all revolutions, including my own.
I walked, ensnared by the grace
of this beautiful, sad, tired city.

Then, turning into a small street,
I noticed the line, and a kiosk
with a window of apples and oranges,
a small mound of apples, red,
stunted, gnarled, but to my eye
more than inviting—miraculous!

Nor did I need the word.
I had the image before me,
holier than the word, above
syllables or music, an existence
by itself: I had only to point.
I approached, pointed, six apples
tumbled into my extended hat
for a ruble, with some change.
God had indeed guided me here.

Walking along, I cleaned one
against my coat, to hell with germs.
If an apple-inflicted death
were mine in Leningrad, let it come,
at the edge of the lovely Neva,
in Pushkin's proud city.
I bit into it, warts and all,
nectar of the day, a red gift
far from home, the Universal Apple!

FIFTH AVENUE

I followed those rounded gorgeous
buttocks for several happy streets:
sailor on a tilting deck (me) –
tightrope over the Falls (she) –

Automobiles stopped in their tracks,
suicides hesitated and were lost,
the frieze over St. Patrick's door
shifted, groaned for a better look.

Her wings quivering, she brushed me,
someone (at last!) yelled Fire –
with the pavement hot, the glass melting,
it was time to get out of town.

LEXINGTON AVENUE

I can't help
the couple embracing
on the corner—
she's in tears,
he's holding her close,
what can the city do
but keep moving?

She's threatening
suicide, or simply
refuses to cook dinner.
He can't fathom
her public emotion
but loves her
nevertheless.

The subway below,
the plane above,
traffic everywhere
and dodging footsteps—
her tears are
the quietest news
in the city.

Prometheus Statue
(Radio City)

Beneath his glare, the artificial flame,
table awnings spawn a tide of sails,
white, green, red, striped and flared.
In summer, the fountain keeps him cool.

He's tamed now: he who stole fire
from the gods is now a tourist trap.
Brightly scoured, in a new coat of paint,
he's more a ballet dancer than a thief.

From Iowa or Rome, strangers stare
between sips of iced tea and the sun.
What do these hatted chattering dears
know of fire, or gods, or classic danger?

And one, lighting a cigarette, flips
the flaming match into the metal hair.

POCKET PARK—EAST SIDE

Listening
as the artificial waterfall
pours down the side
of a building.
Bird on a branch sways,
listening,
astonished, not daring
to sing.

Pegasus on 10th Avenue

Pegasus
my winged horse,
flying Red Horse
of Mobil,
what the hell are you doing
on 10th Avenue?

As long as you're
here on earth,
winged but grounded,
I wish
you were a dray horse
pulling
a cart of vegetables
or children,
an ordinary horse,
weary,
flea-bitten,
flatfooted.

WALL STREET

George Washington
looking down
the Treasury Building steps
is not surprised
at the madness of money in the air.

Didn't he have a house
in Mount Vernon
with possibly a mortgage,
and didn't Martha
want new clothes
and a better visiting carriage?

The good bourgeois
saw the street
as an expanded way of life:
property, private enterprise,
and a well-tended dollar.

George
looking bravely
down Wall,
father of us all ...

The Meeting
for Aaron Kramer

Our hair thinner, otherwise fit,
we meet at the artificial waterfall
splashing down the concrete wall,
a pocket park in the city's stone—
two poets, ammunition spent
on the right things in the wrong time,
nevertheless cheerful: we're still alive.

I say, "Even an artificial waterfall
has something for the soul and ear."
He replies, "Another generation
and who'll remember the real thing?"
We exchange memos, small ambitions.
There is between us an unacknowledged
feeling of keeping the past alive.
We keep our battle scars hidden,
our eyes have a secret praise.

A girl moves by, shimmering, her step
at once dissolves the web. We lean
toward music now, even the fake
waterfall seems in place.
"Lovely perfume, farewell," I say.
"Poetry ever onward!" he grins,
and departs into the common world.

I continue down the street
into the dense forest, birds
swarming everywhere in the foliage,
and deeper on, the real water.

THE RIVER
for Nancy Steinson

Placed not merely by nature
but art, a more difficult arrangement,
we walked across your river of stones.
Unheard, it flows silently by
between the shapes of steel
(boulders older than the Universe)
created by human hands,
durable, yet weightless,
something music understands.

Whether your river is a vision
or actually flowing in the plaza,
the answer lies within a landscape,
serene in downtown traffic,
your secret once, and now ours.

III. ELEGY
(*for Hedda*)

The night has come that I had feared,
the night of timelessness for one,
and a ticking clock for the other.

The dark has come while I stood numb,
the dark which called you in.
I shivered in the light.

The silence came disguised as death,
it robbed all things of speech,
while I stood numb.

Then His step, soft as air,
and a voice, "I am late."
The hour had finally come.

～～

The day rose up cold as doom,
your poor heart labored. I stood
at the door, stared in at the room;
you were far away.

The day held fast, and swayed.
Your poor heart labored. I stood
at the door, your heart faltered,
then your breath flew past
toward a destination unforeseen.

～～

The clock is ticking …

Where are you, my darling?
The clock is a ghostly heartbeat.
Are you as still as this house?
Do you sleep in your narrow house?

The hill is now your home,
eternity's clock is all the furniture,
it ticks but once each century,
an hour is a millennium.

I will leap beyond you soon
and meet you, impossibly,
in a house of wind. Already

the wind is forming the walls
of our house. With patience,
a roof, a door, will appear.

～～

I sleep in our bed,
severed from you, an uprooted heart.
Mysteriously you left me.
There was a violent storm,
and you were gone.

I rise in the night.
All is still. The moon
struggles in the sky,
having lost its sun.
                      Even as I.

Something is about to speak.
Is it a tree, a stone, a star?
Something must be explained,
or justified; someone must speak
and bring news, an error
about to be corrected, a life
rediscovered, restored.

Time pulses and dims,
a week has passed.
It seems I am rooted
while all the universe
swirls, and you, too,
in some cosmic dance
far from the maps
by which I move.

～～

Each morning I put on
that second cup of coffee,
knowing you won't drink it
but wanting it before you
as I drink mine.

You are the steam rising
over the cup, you are mist
rising there in the kitchen:
my darling, what can I do?
What have I done? not done?
Have I left out prayer,
exorcism, miracle?
                None.
None to do the impossible,
to convert mist into flesh.

～～

I long to share your darkness,
the endless journey of the dead.
My heart lies there already,
I feel that sleep within me.
                    Sleep
of a man turning to stone,
or air, or a music known
to those who leave behind
the other, earthly music.

The Last Decade

Breath of a running animal,
of lovers, breath of a forest,
of multitudes, of a shout,
of sibilance, of whispers,
breath of the froth of waves.

Breath of smallest volume,
an ounce, a teaspoon,
my poor breathless one
who sleeps beyond oxygen …

～～

Not to be revoked, not
to be retraced, not
to be undone, not
ever reborn, returned,
made warm again, not
ever shaped again
for kisses, caresses,
never, forever, through
swarm of galaxies, eons,
millennia, never, never
to be returned.

～～

It's a sunny beautiful day.
How I dreaded the arrival
of days such as these!
I want a drab landscape,
days of cloud and rain,
an oblivion along with nature—
but it's sunny and your face
floats above me, serene,
indifferent, free.

Can the rose exist
without her breath?

There must be one rose missing
since she herself is missing,

Or one sunset never repeated,
or one sigh never heard.

And the footstep, hers,
solitary, missing.

～～

I feel your fading breath
within me, becoming my power,
my hope; somehow your death
has lifted me—
            a puzzle
I've yet to reconstruct.

You now have the strength of
darkness; if it keeps you,
I must make peace with it,
even borrow from it.

～～

Faces everywhere,
swarms of mouths and eyes.
Can you possibly be hiding,
anonymous, in this jungle?

What joy to find you here,
there, elsewhere—no matter
except it be a likeness of you,
the remotest chance of you,
a wild dream of you
that my sinking heart
knows is a lie.

How can I wake with the sun,
and you asleep, never to waken?
The immovable tree
breathes, the earth trembles,
the dead moon reflects light,
but you are still, timeless.
I must live with time,
that weight of hours.

What shall I do
with these days and weeks,
absurd calibrations of time?

How shall I shut out
the staring calendar and clock,
and news of daily wars?

With you outside of life,
and I inside, an embryo
waiting to be reborn.

～～

At last comes the knowledge
that the circle is closed,
she within it, forever imprisoned,
I without, forever disbelieving.

The body dissolves, merciful
to the departed, merciless to those
who must remain.   I beat
against that circle; serene
in its power, it hears nothing.
We whose art gave it beauty,
it scorns and gives us nothing.

One of us is fading.
Is it you or I? Are we fading
into something that is both?
I feel within my breath
another breath, my pulse
a double music, my heart
eight-chambered, driving
blood enough for both.
We are recognizable only
to one another, and thrive on that.

～～

Some afternoons, a wind
brushes my arm—or is it you?
All's invisible, all heavy
with meaning. The earth is
indifferent, we feel our way.

You who once was among us
now have become our shadow,
you caress us with darkness.
We are happy with the dark,
with the wind, yet a hand
reaching, touching, invisible,
would be the authentic miracle.

This gnawing doubt,
doubt of time, the event itself,
of my place in the frame ...
                              Death
in his imperturbable truth
has played his single card and left,
while you remain a drifting moon
severed from all gravity,
from the pull of my life,
from the possibility of error,
from the fact, the event itself.

I'm sitting at my desk,
thinking of you: if only
you knew how comforting
to have you close, this balm
which almost brings on peace.

Nothing is said, all is felt,
all known, the fact accepted.
Death, that cunning master
who outwitted god, has left
a link between those who loved.
You carry that filament,
flame of the departed.
While I'm seated at my desk,
waiting for the mail,
a whirl of life in my head,
and you at my ear, smiling.

~ ~

You've freed me
by your departure—it seemed thus,
except I'm chained even tighter
to your ghost. Did you want that?
You could have had me as close
always. I was yours always.

You are in our room when I wake,
a web that won't be brushed away,
that self-repairs, spun out of night,
of gossamer, mysterious renewal.

~ ~

I climb out of the pit,
I fall in again. Weather
seems to be the catalyst;
rain is welcomed somehow,
then bright sunshine; mist
brings a gentle sadness,
the earth's natural condition,
with rain my best companion.

Time is the stone,
water running over the stone,
time is the leap to nowhere.

I hear a door closing.
It is done, O lost companion,
you on one side, I on the other.

The jury was out for months,
It now brings in the verdict:
I am to travel alone. How

fortunate the journey is brief
from this point! You were
the flash, the warning, and I

to wake to the moon waning,
in the minutes remaining.

∽∽

Morning. Movement of planets.
Relentless, this reappearance.
It all comes round again
but we do not.

                You have been,
you are no more; I am,
and you may rest within me,
you may feed upon me;
we feed upon one another.

I have a miraculous Braille
that translates your Having Been
into I Am. On some days
there is We.

The Last Decade

There are no maps in her kingdom,
no houses where she dwells,
or beds, or laughter; a land
without boundary.
                    There she lives,
unknowing of her fate, of time;
she rests in the vale of non-being.

Pain, her truest companion,
is fled, she has no one,
yet I may reach her,
create a world for her
just inside the zone of madness.
We visit, talk, comfort one another.
We are punished by memory,
yet cherish what once included us,
whatever still binds us.

These are fields of nirvana,
real to us, a dream to others.

⁓ ⁓

I'm drawn to my dream poems,
dreams of you, as I walk
the streets, now dream streets.

These are my greetings, my terrors,
mostly little tremors of love,
beamed toward your shadowed world.

I'm drawn to impossibilities,
the farthest edges of mind,
where hope and darkness are at war.

I find you there, obscure angel,
created of your once aliveness,
which I guard with all my power.

And you, responding by silence,
guard me. Thus our half-life,
vivid as perpetual sunset.

I turned the corner, stopped,
stared out into transparent air.
I kept my lips together
to keep my smile a secret,
but the music of you spilled over,
and again that twin surprise:
joy of recognition, and heartbreak
that you exist only in my imagining.

How shall I cope with this?
I'm waiting for time to instruct me.
We must be one, two become one,
doomed in that amber light,
entwined as bark and tree,
as lilac and its sweet perfume,
as night and its comforting.

～～

A great peace is over me.
Have I died? Yet I sit
within my room, in a chair;
months have fallen from my shoulders.

The peace is reconciliation.
I'm reconciled with time,
distance, pain, whatever's done
or will to be done. I wait as a stone.

I'm human still. The air
burns upon my skin. They say
I can see her quite soon,
it's a journey of merely a day.

She is adrift in a constellation
near the sun. The region is warm.
The journey should be a happy one.
She is warm; we have a heartbeat.

The Spring solstice arrives.
The earth tilts gently
so as not to disturb you.
You ride along with her,
and I with you, a single journey.
What's lost between us in time
is reconciled in space.   Sweetly
we ride together, a destination
unknown to all the living, and
once unalive, known forever.

～～

You within me, haunting me
like an ectoplasmic glow,
a form of life outside of life,
a nourishment I learn to savor.

This transmuted power
is at my fingers, guides my poem.
I demolish all reason,
inhaling you, a constant vapor.

Amorphous, without shape,
you are around me, within me,
beyond air, food, or water,
a constant violet light.

～～

Will you visit me, sweet memory?
Will you appear and embrace me?
How the living need the dead!

The departed, free and absolved,
know the days of those left behind,
their inconsolable regrets,
a knowledge not to be revealed,
and knowing all, knowing all,
yet unable to speak.

Night again. Where are you,
my sweet unalive darling?
Night that engenders memory,
that demon notebook, speak.

Night with its leaves and terrors,
its indefinable loneliness,
that cloak of suffocation;
come, tender ghosts, I welcome
even the cruel ones.

All that were hers, mine, ours;
all welcome in their darkness,
the long succession of nights to come,
nights of the moon, white as her arms,
come, all, if there is news of her.

～～

The curtain rustles. I know
it's merely the wind, and know
the wind is of this world.

But the wind's origin
is unknown; it may be
from another earth, another

terrestrial habitation
where metaphors are born
and come to the poet's call.

Perhaps wind comes to my bidding,
wind of this world, born
of yet another, exhausted

by the journey from Orion
and carrying a single word:
you, you, you.

The Last Decade

Today I weakened,
no reason I can think of ;
a weakness somewhere in the body.
I had to sit, and then tears.
Once again, the finality
that each day affirms.

I'll tell no one … even if I could.
It will pass, it's already
moving away, a streak of weather
into a new softer pattern.

The Last Decade

IV. LOSSES & SILENCE

LOSSES

Loss of letters, such as one
that befell me, letter of a darling;
its loss like the actual person
has added to a weight of grieving,
token once loved, and hoarded,
left on a bus in a cold city,
never to be returned neither
for sentiment nor show of pity—

compare with the loss of written pages,
fiction built with a house of cards,
a dense tangle of intricate webbing
untangled, words on a yellow pad
broke my heart, lost to a world
uncaring of words, or my anguish,
like a melody uncharted
from the soul of the departed—

last of the year, a loss of warmth,
of the glittering green serpent round my neck,
wool spun from her generous fingers,
an old scarf, companion of winters,
lost forever on the Long Island Railroad!
Neither of these found, though reported,
dear to me for inarticulate reasons:
letter, script, scarf, now visions.

SILENCE

The tree, once a commonplace,
now comforts me with its wisdom;
odor of leaf and bark surrounds me,
flows into feeling, fellowship,
a strange companion for the journey.

Once I clung to father and mother
until I left them clinging
to one another; then they fell,
as final leaves in farewell,
the puzzle intact, lingering.

I take note, this morning,
of the sparrow's chatter on his branch,
amusing my cat at the window: they know
something I may have overlooked.
Revelation comes by chance.

I listen to nothing but my breath.
I shake the tree, knowledge
responds with silence, and waits.
That wind again: could it be death?

END OF THE WORLD

It might even be painless
(seen as an entertainment),
from a white peak in the Himalayas
to a skiing party in Utah or several
sure-footed mountain goats who lost their way.

In short, an event not totally
unobserved.
              And somewhere,
under a stone or abutment,
beneath a waterfall or on the wings
of a monarch butterfly, a flash
(possibly an outcrop of mica)
is trying to tell us something—
we're gone, a passing shadow,
whisper of flame, the instant fossil.

Triptych for Hedda

1. *The Cemetery*

Your name, an implanted shadow
on the stone, is with me as a brand.
At first, it was a burden of stone
that crumbled into powder, then
into something the sun absorbs,
a mist of days, a residue of time.

Your name and its five letters
ring within me like tiny chimes,
heard by no one but myself;
chimes, or soft bells, or voices.

These mortal games carry us
drifting as pollen, deathward,
a dark flowering of souls,
flesh into shadow, shadow into stone.

2. *Spring Blossoms*

They've returned again, darling,
at our window, a whim of nature
renewing life to one form of life
and not the other.
                    I must accept
this imperious, blind decree.
They had not chosen to appear
but accepted the same cold decree,
imperious, beyond appeal.

What stirs in me is a slumbering hope
that blossoms, returning here, may mean
your return elsewhere, places
unknown to me but spoken of.
I embrace these blossoms, dear,
as you may somewhere be embraced,
a dream we long to share with plants.

3. The House Plant

Because it breathes, and you do not,
I see it as your other life;
I stop to water it, and touch
the leaves or brush away the dust.

It's here, in our room, a presence
as durable as yours, serene,
another blessed form of nature.
It keeps the chlorophyll refreshed,
as I keep your memory.

What it knows, and I cannot,
is the sense of millennia,
circle of time, of the flaming sun
itself encircled: encirclement
that widens out, and is sustained,
gathering all in its warmth.

The plant secretes life, a gift
denied to you which I accept
as though it were a gift to me.

The Dead Think Only of their Bodies

The dead think only of their bodies.
The anguish not of departure
but the disposition of effects:
the closet full of unwanted shoes,
that page of revision, there, on the
corner of the desk, I implore,
beg you to destroy
for my sleep's sake.
                    My body
from bed to casket, that arm
dragging, lift it, lift it, please!
The fear (even then) of falling …

Whether the arms are crossed
or the hands correctly clasped,
whether the face is smoothed,
hair in place: the departed
will forever be agonized
by a twitching eyelid, exposed
genitalia, the fear (even then!)
of not hearing a whispered farewell,
and most fearful, the unbearable
contents, never to be known,
of a last unopened letter.

Red

Of blood, or a wound
of the blood itself;
an agony of red,
color of estrangement, despair,
roses bred of the vine, the air;
reminders of red.

Most interior of flesh,
yet outermost eye,
each red a bursting sun,
its heat as color,
the cool heat of death.

One wishes to embrace,
to eat the red petal by petal,
or in one insane engorgement
to have that color, that heat,
that perfection,
within.

Alice Baber, artist

1. *Lenox Hill Hospital*

Your headdress of steel
against the pale skin:
is this a galactic visitor
landed in a hospital bed
instead of a pastel meadow?

We know it's you, Alice,
disguised perhaps, but the smile tells;
your arms and legs hidden
but all your fingers waving;
your forehead as I remember it,
lips and mouth in a doll's shape.

Death and life are everywhere,
and here, somehow, you give off life,
as light upon the window, of the eye,
even as your voice has that tremor.
You tire quickly, drift toward sleep.
I say goodbye, turn at the door, and leave.
Your light stays on my orange sweater.

2. *In her house, after her death*

Seated at her kitchen table,
we open a bottle of wine and say
nothing; we enter her non-being.
As the back door, the shedding tree
leans with its autumn weight.
The sky is all in Baber blue,
the reds and violets of sunset,
earth drifting with her colors.

The Last Decade

We are in her workroom, moving
among pans and dishes, jars
of her jams, scattered memos,
tubes of paint uncapped.
We try the jam, read the memos,
to share this lost life with her.
We arrange the brushes and tubes,
our ridiculous order of the living,
and stare at an unfinished canvas
rigid within the frame.

The plastic glasses, filled with color,
are lined across the shelves,
paint dissolved into water;
the alchemy of Alice
in every room, white canvas
afloat into skies of Tiepolo,
her faceless, wingless cherubim
riding in a joyous firmament;
those blues, pinks, and yellows,
a beatitude of pulsations
reaching across a galaxy,
heartbreak without end.

Death of a Magician

If he couldn't work his way
out of those cunning chains,
what chance had I?
                None at all.
And yet, the thought itself, the sheer
fact of trying to outwit Him
takes the fancy.
              And I see
far ahead in the silent calendar
(wink of an eye), as in a wood
gargantuan with oaks, and behind
each tree His shadow spilled
between my running steps—

and turning, I'd throw my bolt,
a handkerchief of linked colors,
a hatful of white rabbits
to slow Him down but He came on
in a dark cloud, stumbled, and plucked
the last cry from my throat.

What a chase! I'm still trembling,
my black cape gone, and in its place
a flutter of white wings.

Music

Shaken free of sleep,
the music of sleep follows me,
lingers within my blood,
overwhelms the hours,
and though the day roars
like a furnace, I'm lifted
into the great curve of silence,
that rack music is stretched upon
to yield its true sound;
it sweetly beckons a peace
whirling at the edge of time,
serenely confident, holy,
the idea of an ending
often called death.

BABY WHALE IN CAPTIVITY

I miss the sea most of all.
It took me some weeks
to realize the whitewashed pool
was not my true home:
the water too transparent,
without mystery or danger,
and my mother's shadow
no longer moved about me.
How I missed her hovering
bulk, her weight of
tenderness! I slept
in peace beneath her fins.

Then somewhere within me
her loss, like a wound,
opened and spread
and pulled me away
in a tide darker than the sea.

V. THE TRANCE OF EROS

A. The Wound

The Last Decade

I will not look beyond the day.
Let the night come and go.
Whoever may be with her,
let him be; I've cut that part
as one cuts a nerve. I'll keep
some other grip upon her heart.

I keep sight of her fitfully
as though it were all an apparition.
She moves through kitchens, halls,
I'm not sure whether to follow.
Is that coffee still warm,
and the bed with its whispers?

There's a hunger beyond food
will break the body, even music
gives no sustenance, nor time.
One prays for sleep, for meaning,
it doesn't matter: love betrays
even as it keeps us breathing.

When she broke the news:
bombshell!
               I'm still
picking out the splinters.
Signs of concussion remain,
dizzy spells, a vacant stare:
nothing on the surface
to frighten a neighbor,
but the damage was there.

The shape of loss, at first,
is simply absence; some force
akin to gravity disrupted.
Venus the planet off its track.
It took some weeks before
the landscape settled back.

Then the vine upon the wall
came into focus
with the one remembered rose
missing.

The Last Decade

There were initial signs
my poor mind did not decipher,
so certain I stood in her favor.
After a voyage and return,
where else to be welcomed back
but in her arms? And they
responded, or seemed to ...

It was not until your clothes
came off, and I at your breasts
fainting and delirious,
that I sensed the change,
but not enough to slow me
toward your heated body.

I could not stop, nor care
whether you responded or not.
I was there at the central core
of all my longing.
I had your body then.
The shock would come later.

The Last Decade

At night, during sleep, he cannot
endure the playbacks of desire,
her breasts dipping over him,
his teeth upon her, his mouth
covering hers, his tongue upon her,
now their kisses and seizures,
her mouth now upon him
and like birds their chattering
flooded the hours, the room,
induced a sleep from which
he at least hoped never to waken.

The Last Decade

On an evening walk, alone,
I pass the window of the room
where we would lay in afternoons
of joy, jolted by our flesh, seared
by some internal heat that flared
and simmered like the Borealis …

Now, with the window dark,
I fight the image of other bodies
upon that same bed of darkness.
He the thief and she the cunt,
replacing me the lover and she the beloved,
replacing the room of our hushed music
with a room of the thrusting cock,
kiss of my soul with kiss of their newness,
cry of my elation to his mere whispering.

And if the window's lighted,
I see that glare wherein we met,
where light was dark and dark a heaven,
where dark illumed, and love blinded,
and light took what dark had given,
and light rang out with innocence.
Room of my created light,
all in that room, haunted
forever by earlier voices,
where watching books astonished
at new fingers at their pages …

With the curtains closed, my mind's
as dark as hell, and raging.

The Last Decade

Am I saved? Has it passed?
But soon the furies re-enter:
yours, they say, yours, yours!
Is she mine? The proof of kisses
is made of breath, of air.
What's owned may drift away.
I write my words to wish away
her spirit, but those kisses
that once accelerated with my heart,
quickened with my pulses to urge me,
guide me, curl me within her,
each kiss a rapid yes,
the yes I once took as truth,
her yes of the gospel, of goodness,
the yes of my gathering,
yes of my coming ...

And her arms, light as surprise,
reaching up around my neck—
things she's now forgotten.

The Last Decade

That you have changed, or wished
to change, is yours to do.
Fade, then, out of mercy.
I can deal with memory
easier than your presence.
Your presence, that welcoming smile,
I could only now suspect,
as I now suspect your goodness.
I'd rather see you from afar
and get the news that you're well,
and happily alive without me.

(That last thought, once
undreamed of, now at hand …)

The street. We stand and talk.
And now deception must be done:
she's off to visit with a friend.
Well, isn't he a friend?
A fornicatious friend, the friend
who supplants a first friend,
while she may look to a third …

Wrong. But it's new territory,
one longs to be suspicious.
She says, I will love you always.
But the crime is admitted!
She has confessed … within her rights!
She has the right, as a woman.
Yes, of course, each owns himself
but may use others. And so,
the civilized beast (us) must go
to play the beast with another.
Even as you. Or I. Or us.
Then go. Do it. Forget other.
Let other wait it out.
Time heals all intensities.
But this one devours Time.
Time is out of it here.
Only sun and cloud, cold rain,
the wound aching in every weather.

Darling (from afar), sleep is impossible.
My head's alive with exhausting images,
haunted questions and no answers,
I'm in a maze, those corridors all
lead to shock, perhaps knowledge.
I need revelation: how I envy the saints!

I'm baffled by your power.
You do nothing but exist.
You move in a green background
which I translate as the coverlet
of your bed: O that green,
green of the bedsheet, green plants
hanging, chlorophyll everywhere,
green of the vine across the windowsill
coiling around me as I try to sleep.

In the market checkout counter
the beasties meet (she and I),
she well-fucked, I in hunger,
we try to keep a friendship going.
Perfumed female of the species,
she's marvelous in pretending
nothing is wrong, that I can
want her smile and not her body.
Is she a fool? Not at all.
Women are the proof of pragmatism.
Their souls bend, rarely break.
Their minds are fixed upon
a sensual beam, a homing glide.

Let it be. Lightning has struck.
Who will notice my charred clothes?
Not she. That film upon her eyes,
some dripped mascara—would it were tears!

I cross the street to avoid her,
then cross over to intercept.
I long to feel that stab of remorse,
a loss never to be replaced.
We nod, ask the social questions,
and I add (fool!) "You look beautiful,"
to which she replies, "So do you."

Is this the way madness comes on?
I want, at that moment, there,
in the sunlight, to kiss her breasts,
open her blouse and risk arrest,
kiss each amid falling houses
and exploding streets.
                        I breathe,
I stand close, and brush her arm.
"Then you'll come by for coffee?"
To ask me inside the door,
to let the hurricane in …

God no! Where her glance alone
dropped me to one knee. I tell you
I once drew blood from those lips.

A day of sunshine—joy!
She's out of sight, out of mind.
Stay away, I'm free this day.
I speak her name, not a ripple
of pain: this must be peace or death.

Ahead, the street, her window ...
But the news in my head is good.
I breathe great draughts of memory:
In bed, nude, vodka and Dickens,
we'd hear street sounds
outside the window.
     She'd say,
"What a foolish world out there.
If they only knew!" We loved then,
O sweet embraces with her yes
whispering me down the atmosphere
and we'd blaze out like falling stars.
Afterwards, small talk, we're
bathed in our wisdom, pure usage
of the dragon Time, tame as a cat,
our bed companion.
     We're ignorant
of the hours, we're adrift
on the afternoons of desire,
out to sea without a compass.
North is within us, quivering;
we're the only North, and warm
while the whole street shivers.

The Last Decade

The point is, there's no blame.
She's meant it to mean something else,
a gentle diminution of feeling,
not this fury I try but cannot
press down.
         Still, I hide it from her.
"We don't own one another …"
The jargon of the day wins.
We own none, no one, nothing.
We are nada, a creature of
non-believing. The microscopic
cells collide and race away,
to fuse and split again …

What began as a gleam of desire
leaped to the flesh of endearment.
Let it go. Too late. Give her
to the other, the unnamed conspirator.
While they sweat, oblivious,
I'll move upon them, a chill wind;
he'll think the window's open;
she'll know it's me, a desperate ghost.

The Last Decade

Can she be honest and say,
I love you now and have always?
What does it mean? Does she
want two or four? Is the woman
suddenly awakened to this?
Even (you'll say) as men are?

That's the façade. The truth is …
She's found a fresh heart,
a closer one, a better cock,
all's fair in love and cockery,
and the matchstick castle
(love's only construction)
comes tumbling down. You
can't build it twice, not
with the same matchsticks.
The tired heart whispers:
How many such passions
have I left? Arms that held you
now drop, however the greeting.
It has died. (And possibly
I, my darling, with it.)

The Last Decade

My dear, what have I done?
I've aged, of course. I've had
only half a life to give—did you
hope, somewhere, for a full one?
I would give not half but whole.
How could this have been predicted,
your chance encounter with another?
I'd left you unguarded, was that it?
I'll never know. It can't be told.

Let her go. It's lost anyway.
Her yes of love I'd long to die with.
And now, out of the yes, the revelation
that she could unlove me,
could turn, and go.

Should I wish you well?
And if I wished you ill,
nothing would be gained for me,
I'd be unhappier still
because of your own unhappiness.
Be well, then, without me.
I'm like a sixth finger
on the glove, I'm a third
in the large world of twos.
Musical chairs have pushed me out:
all lovers are seated but me.
Yet chairs may go round again ...
(Dear God, how dreamers dream!)

Now time, like a skinner's knife,
has cut the pelt from the carcass.
It's a painful howling air
at first upon the skin; soon
however, the days secrete an ointment
much like nature's gum
over a tree's rough wound,
and the muscles flex and move,
the membranes knit together.

Weather returns; all things
in mist are joined; memory
tries to set the heart in order.
But desire wrecks the house.
Starlight seen through the roof,
a blind universe speeding away …

Light has touched and flown.
Something new must come.

What comes is benign indifference.
Time's knife is now time's balm,
curer of the wound born of time.

The blood resumes its slow course,
the pulse to shallower soundings.
The body's no longer mysterious.

See how the lame walk again,
those eyes no longer in pain,
nor the day any longer blessed.

I breathe, she breathes,
but we breathe apart.
We've lost our synchronous hearts.

But earth's still ringed with fire.
How I'd wish to return again,
if only to burn, to burn!

A month of hours, like snow,
has buried the landscape.
A strange quiet upon the body,
a quiet allowing one to hear
the soft hammers of the blood.

Even the window to that room
is neither light nor dark,
but reflecting a tone of each,
as an accustomed discord in music.
I feel the beginning of distance,
a blessed weightlessness:
weight above and weight under
now equalized.

                I have broken
free of the iron field, broken
from the centrifugal arc into …
shall I call it peace?

Then I ask (a dread request)
to drop by for some books.
Passing her room, the door ajar,
the bed touches off an alarm,
green coverlet where we moved
and gripped and spoke our promises.
How to shut that sound forming, hurry,
before the coverlet leaps into flame!
I gasp, my ears drumming, rush
to the door.
              "What is it?"
"I'm ill"… and down the stairs,
to the air, singed, barely alive.

She who said love, love,
she who swore yes, yes,
whose eyes closed under my kisses,
called me back from the dead,
who kept me locked within her
after my fierce joy had fled,
until our skins, coated with sweat,
would cool in the summer air,
and still she kept me within her,
within our sleep.   Her magic
a prolongation of desire, now
rising as the skinner's knife,
that paradise reborn as hell.

I am now there, and Time,
that I once laughed at,
now laughs at me; it knows
that love, once fled, consigns
a man to a diminished life.
O never to cross back again!
All paths are blocked.
Thus it is with voices, until
between lip and ear
even the whisper is lost.
Where *I love* becomes mere syllables,
as a remark about weather,
and then the language dims,
the inner mind allows
just enough room to move,
and wait for the dark.

Light has touched and flown.
Something new must come.

B. Biography For Ipsithilla
(After Catullus)

Amabo, mea dulcis Ipsithilla.
meae deliciae, mei lepores ...
  — Catullus

1.

In the marketplace, amid jars and ointments,
Her perfume rushed toward me. I turned.
A steady-eyed, half-smiling woman,
Toenails painted, eyelids darkened with oil,
Her loose flowing robe broken
By the double curve of her breasts—
She turned as I did, giving a slight shrug
Of her shoulders, almost disdainfully.
Her buttocks shifting in a faint rhythm.
Was she queen or slut? Either, I thought,
Would be a find. I followed to her door.
She was alone and allowed me to enter.
The time was ready to test the miracle
Or let it fade. "My tunic bid me to come,"
I said, and smiled, fearing instant death.
But Eros, double-dealing, stayed her arm
And touched her thigh. Our hands locked,
Our lips followed, my flesh grew
(As if some swift tumultuous plant)
And burst within her. She murmured her name.
Ipsithilla.

2.

You say, Ipsithilla, you've heard of our philosophers
But are not impressed. "I have my own thoughts,"
You exclaim, stroking your dog while eating grapes.
Indeed you have. You speak of the Ceasars
As though they were chariot pullers, suggesting
A single dancing girl could undo the lot.
Of Archimedes' wish to move the world, you remark
It would be a waste of the world's time.
One should stay indoors most of the day
And find indoor pleasures, is your maxim.
A believer in the Fates, you take my presence
As a command from Eros which must be obeyed.

I nod at these divine insights, and trust
All that she prepares, food or potion,
That leads to love's awakening. For her science,
Lucretius, if he knew, would come running.

3.

If you could see my disordered afternoon
When you choose housekeeping instead of my arms!
I'm morose, forget my manuscripts,
Even the chariot-racers can't lure me out.
Won't your floor wait? And the washing?
Why this weekly flurry in the kitchen?
It's against all logic except a woman's.
I blame your cruelty, possibly your humor.

Ipsithilla, you must know I hunger
For your body, that arching delight,
As much as your cakes and bread.
O gods, must the house be cleaned?
Yes. It's Lunae, and I must wait.

4.

Another birthday, and you don't seem
At all bothered. Time hurries around you,
But you seem unhurried, unhearing.
You dye your nails and hair, you say
A woman's age is perfectly clear
And should be told outright if not seen.
Indeed, you carry whatever age you have
As easily as an animal her pride:
You take it for granted, a boon to man
And a delight to the gods.

As Heraclitus knew, all things are one thing,
Though they change. Your birthday is one year,
Or possibly ten. We ourselves are two,
Yet one. And kisses, dear Ipsithilla,
Those uncounted whispers of the soul,
Days of the infinity of days, you take
Merely as a reasonable event, and forget.
Therefore, if your date of birth bores you,
May I secretly salute your mother?
It was she, after all, who linked our Fates,
And I'd feel this homage justified.

5.

That dog, my dear, the one you fondle
There in your lap—let him go.
You stroke the smooth belly, you touch
His nose, mouth, ear—a mere dog!—
But your fingers turn him into a creature
I'm jealous of. I have known
Your fingers at my temple, at my thigh,
Those fingers touch my life and death.
Shall an animal be thus anointed?

I beseech you, let the dog go.
I'm here, waiting, smoldering,
Ready to turn to flame. Call me,
I'll come running, barking. I can beg, too,
But will make you pay for that.

6.

You're very thoughtful today, Ipsithilla.
I've suggested several unusual copulations
But you lie on your stomach unsmiling.
You're not amused when I bite your ear.
On mentioning Corinna, you stir slightly,
And say she's a slut, hardly a victory.

I'm aroused by the heat.
Ipsithilla will not be moved. Is she hungry?
Is she bored? Angry? I yearn for her,
With or without her responding passion.
Her flesh is all I want today.
She'll moan, grit her teeth, weep.
I won't be put off. There are such days
When punishment for one or both
Is the best we can have.

7.

Insisting she has no clear idea of her character,
Ipsithilla exclaims: I am nothing, I am many
And none, I have no sense of myself through the day.

I'm unaware she is anything but herself,
Though she protests. Is it a mask in which
To hide her wickedness? I watch her more carefully,
More secretly, but always, when I call her name,
She turns and is indeed herself. It's I who wonder
Of my own self, if I exist only by her grace.
If she is nothing, then who am I in her arms?
If I come not to find her, what then brings me?
Enough of these women's preposterous thoughts.
I continue to stalk her, possess her, ghost or flesh,
And let the idle poets tell me why.

8.

Ipsithilla reaches demurely under my tunic,
Murmuring alarm: Will this fit inside me?
Oh no, you won't, you wouldn't be that cruel!
But she can't wait to let me enter, greedily
Set to grip and groan to my thrusting flesh.
This game of my savagery is one she enjoys.

Eros has made you so cunningly a companion,
So tuned your spirit, this obvious art
And inner design, all fused in your eyes
That reflect light but let the body in.
Your games and my meditations, my words
And your silences, a sleep, a death, a spasm—
Are these the large events of this Roman age,
Amid the wars and our thirsting lips?

9.

I watch you fall asleep, even as you turn,
Exhausted after love making, or was it possibly
The wine that left you drugged and sluggish?
Often, when locked in love's thrashing power,
You'd praise our good use of energy—
Energy used thus was the wisest, you'd say.
Would Socrates dare to argue further?

Asleep, you clasp the pillow like a child.
Your breathing is deep, your body trusting.
One could imagine you in a lion's cage,
Your sleep around you like a shield.
Are you safe from the eyes of this lustful city?
But such dangers, Ipsithilla, you can cope with.
Lions and men live to be tamed.
We're all cornered in that cage of love
Where battles, even if lost, are savored as victories.
Sleep, but be warned. I'll be rested when you wake.

10.

You were totally unpredictable yesterday.
I arrived from the country to find you sulking—
I hate that, it disfigures your soul.
I was silent. We drank wine of Methymna.
You reprimanded me for my tardiness
And the new young boy in my house.
You repeated Corinna was a slut, possibly diseased.
I thought the day was not to be salvaged,
Whereupon—bless your illogic, your mad heart—
You suggested we drown ourselves in love,
Right there, at the moment. Was I agreeable?

Agreeable, Ipsithilla? That endearing question!
Have I not proven it before? Name
The day and hour, be it pain or pleasure,
Whatever brew you have in mind I'll drink, and drown.

11.

Dear Ipsithilla, I trust this letter reaches you
From Genoa where I'm kept on business.
It's the business of gold, a dreary vice,
But often necessary. My mind flies
From this boredom to you. Are you as weary?
Are you staring out upon the streets of Rome,
Looking for my figure in the crowd?
I'd doubt if you'd admit it, my dear.
You're one to keep such feelings to yourself.
Yet I know your thoughts are upon my return,
And I as well, dear friend, have a sharpened desire.
I ask you not to forget our bouts of love,
Our boasts, bruises, and new surprises,
Each thing that binds us to time and place.
For if we have no mooring to those days,
We lose all else, and Rome becomes a desert.

12.

Will it be possible to forget Ipsithilla?
She smiled when once I spoke that secret thought.
She knows her own answer. And yet,
If I could, could ever (aside from death) forget
Those eyes that lead inward to the Garden—
Would I be happier? Can the denial
Be a greater gift than the gift itself?
And if she forget Catullus, would he perish
And be utterly consumed? Combing her hair,
Trusting her mirror, Ipsithilla firmly believes,
Or leads me to believe, that love is best
Unpremeditated and unspoken.
Unspoken, unthought of, kisses spring from air,
And air has neither origin nor end …

But still, will it be possible to forget her?
Even one who forgets the air is doomed to breathe it.
Her voice is pleasurable, and I must breathe.
I can't see myself out of breath or hearing.
Yet I'm haunted by what's uncertain:
This drowning age and a woman's heart.
We drift, we cling, age and heart and she.

The Last Decade

VI. CREDO

Variations on a Willow Tree

1.

What to do with the willow,
burning with autumnal fever,
burning with chemical fire.
Be warned, stay clear!
Helpless the watchers,
joyful the cold wind.

2.

As frost sharpened its breath,
yellow, like a disease,
introduced death as beauty.
Nature's oxidizer, air,
did the rest: branches
into flame, and winter's ash.

3.

Deep within the grain,
the green receding heart
will sleep all winter long.
Earth will draw the blood down.
The willow sways with the earth,
alive to that interior song.

Credo

When first I met the simple leaf,
green, slumbering,
I did not see the universe
though on that branch it hung,
shaped as green, slumbering,
as any mammoth plan
that will not tell its end.

It's the tree that shakes the wind.

Winter Birds

A rush of dark shadows
then the whole willow
weighted down with music—
they should be elsewhere,
far from this pale light
as they flash by
confounding winter.

I'm deployed ahead,
already into Spring
with my human wishes.
Wingless, I see
their small miraculous wisdom:
flight without reason,
the future merely
the song's present echo,
heard now, far ahead,
that frozen day of silence
waiting to explode.

Spring Spider

What did he survive on?
Was air his food? He lay
curled in an ice-bucket, numb
with the long winter and the silence.

The warmth of my breath touched him,
reaches his bones (has a spider bones?)—
whereupon he stirs, those legs
grip the porcelain sides, stretch,
as he starts the climb to the rim.

He finds an angle in the beam
where he'll repair a sagging web
and cast for food. The old game
we both know.
                A taste of blood
to stir the blood. Sooner or later
a fly will show.

Look Who's Here

I know this Spring coming on,
The deceptive sky, blue air,
A stirring deep within the grass,
And though I'm bored with the signs,
I long for the one small leaf
Edging across the brick wall,
The dying spore come to life.
Then the vine will form, grow,
From wall to window, under
And through, thick round
My wrist, a poultice to my brow
Which burns, and cools, and burns.

The Canvas

Cezanne loved apples and oranges;
he understood onions better than people.
Others painted faces, breasts, and buttocks.
Nature has a way with the human creature,
their cereals and fruits in a basket,
miracles overflowing; their suffering
noticed only by light and shade.

The canvas accepts each gift,
wind at the curtain, the absolute
stillness of Vermeer's interior,
Rembrandt's cunning and humanity as one.
Light and shade, the ultimate form,
formless as the waves of the sea.

MATISSE AND THE DOVE
(after Cartier-Bresson)

Held in that human hand,
the dove thinks, "Where am I?
I should be off flying somewhere,
but this man is holy. His hand's a nest."

Matisse, pencil at his sketchpad,
the old man and his art's creature,
thinks, "Who am I? Is the dove
within my hand, or I somehow
growing from the feathers?"

He feels a pulse joining his own,
dreaming upon the simple line,
line to curve, curve to breast,
as the dove nods in sweet repose,
its mystery intact, fully at rest.
And so they stare, stare and think,
white feathers and a white beard,
line to curve, curve to breast,
upholding all the universe.

On Eating the Lake Trout
(for Amanda Palmer)

Thinking back to the line
luring the fish to its doom:
a victim first of need,
and then aesthetics,
as any object loved
is thus devoured ...
                        She is
delighted with the catch,
cold upon the pan,
and later on our plate.

Amanda knows the fish
is no painting,
and must be eaten,
and enjoyed, the lake
notwithstanding.
She knows the trout
is also the evening's color,
devised by her,
even to the pink
beneath the skin,
that beguiling terror.

THE RINGS OF SATURN

Lord, how I run, dazzled by your design,
A dream of impossibility, my sole equation.
And all the while phosphorous burning down,
Odor in my nose, my own bones burning
In an acid of consciousness.
                            I call upon
Jung and Einstein: gear me to that wheel
You've both designed, hub and circumference,
Spinning the soul on a flashing road of light!

Light and time, light and revelation,
The whole universe dangling,
Moving on and out as the heart breaks,
And not a sound, not a sound.

Belles Lettres

Voltaire, busy with his visions,
looked out of the window
and saw the day was good.

He winked at God, dressed,
called his carriage, sped
across Paris to pick up

some choice lots at auction:
God may be a joke but
real estate was bound to rise.

Hurrying back to Candide
and get his dummkopf hero into
Cunegonde's lap, and out again,
to taste the horrors of the world.

The Unfinished Poem

I'd say we were well-matched:
myself calling the shots (so I thought)
and the Poem refusing a new shape
(question of an uncertain verb.)

I set it aside, hoping—as nature
often suggests—we'd be reconciled.
But I learned the poem was outside
of nature, a universe in a bottle
adrift in a lexical sea.

One morning, the poem vanished:
a weariness of the spirit.
Perhaps I had tired of it,
or had it tired of me?
I knew we would meet again,
each in some new disguise,
refusing to be recognized,
the poem refusing to be finished,
impossible to be grasped,
even as mercury, shapeless,
never to be seen as one thing.

Consoling a Young Writer On a Rejection from a Literary Magazine

My friend, poet and naïf,
new to the age of dreamers,
avoid those unsmiling sycophants;
they are forever peeling an onion,
sharpening theses and arrows
or humping their academic brethren
while slowly dying of boredom;
all engaged of climbing the ladder
of enterprise and grim tenure,
eating each other's entrails
while slowly dying of atrophy.

No, they are not our literary kin,
stay clear of them, they deal
in falsity, fakery, quackery
and endless tribal hijinks;
to which I say take thy poems
elsewhere, away from Names and Powers,
obfuscations and residuals.
Stay with the air of Art,
where success and failure are brothers,
and hatreds more moderate
and even forgivable,
where fellowship is the true law
of authors, and struggle shared.

We all must live.
Those who write, those who print;
things are never left to chance;
we choose with whom we dance.

Aspects of Ann

1.

One might say the house
is herself: a mystery
best understood on days
when her plants are greenest
and happily watered. Then
she is happy, with portents
as lightly as curtains lifted
by a distant aureole. She turns
to dispel the rain-filled cloud
with a Cole Porter song,
while I applaud.

2.

This room designated as my castle,
her wall-to-wall creation,
in which I perform my suspensions
while earthbound. From sleep
I rise to her calling, roused
toward happiness. My heart sings.
This time it is she who applauds.

3.

To make love, the making of,
what cannot be made and yet
we labor to construct, knowing
it exists if we're held to the path,
the bond of desire, uncertainty,
to fly without weather warnings
or signs of destination, and arrive;
we feel the arrival ahead,
a blind descent, gift of chance.
In such climate we seem to thrive.

4.

The quickened touch as we pass,
breath of wind or desire,
touch of breast, curve of time,
confirming a bond of the body,
an oncoming trust of the flesh:
this we want and will have.

Sunset on the horizon,
ourselves pulsing in that flame,
and the swift conflagration!

5.

It's over-the-shoulder,
catch-as-catch-can;
you be the lady, I the man.

But as I grow older
and fearful of height,
heaven's easier found on earth.

Be it shoulder or knee,
or the undisclosed heart,
let's keep it always as play, as art.

6.

Morning. Is this another day?
Can we doubt it? The clock insists
it is so, but sleepers, inert, deny
until one leaps from the bedsheets,
whispers a greeting to the waking other,
and angels gone, struggle to the day,
to the self of each, to the love of other,
and the fact that life is here,
to extract kisses and fealty—
but first, waiting, blessed coffee!

7.

Ann in her bath
flesh fair and warm
with Renoir's light
on her flashing arm

Her foot and toes
are carefully done
from there to the torso
where beauty glows

Light of water and air
plays on the skin
an undulation
that runs

quivering, a patina
that paint will keep
while art contains her
all else must wait

8.

A family shadow upon her,
known ghost, a visitor
silent outside the door.

Shadow that endears her;
rush of the dark overwhelms,
sin of the lingering parent.

Coming upon her seated
at a window, sunlight returning
what the spirit has lost.

Strands of a desperate cloth,
there are wounds cannot
be shared, or balm given.

She turns with her quick smile,
mask aside, and her fears,
and my nearest thing to tears.

9.

I think of Adam's fall
caused by an apple:
is Ann a follower of Eve?
Because she loves apples,
eats one before love-making;
does that mean anything
to me, taster of plums and oranges?

With the Garden gone,
the serpent is disrepute,
you'd think the question moot—
but Ann bites so juicily
into the apple, it makes her wiser:
her species dares to eat now
and think on it later.

The new garden, godless,
good and evil entwining bodies,
who's to be sure which will win
or which the original sin?
Meanwhile, the apple entertains.
We each take a bite, red or green,
with God nowhere to be seen.

10.

She's singing off in the kitchen,
slicing the carrots for dinner.
"Bird in a gilded cage!" I call out.
"Bird in a guilty cage!" she laughs.

Dropping a note or two, adding
a trill not in the score,
she sings without reason, a burst
of light and longing.

                        I'm the bird
circling her, my tree of delight.
I sing at night within her branches.

"More Poems! More Poems!"
—letter from Patricia

1.

If one could find that tree of words
to shake again ... but wind had stripped it,
and I must wait for an event
to stir, to raise those sleeping vowels.
Nothing comes without desire
of its coming: imagine love,
a hurricane in a bottle, asleep,
then rushing out to the air.
We wait, and then the call.

When Time's unlocked, and men adrift,
and stars uncertain of their place—
there's the cry *More Poems*
comes to the swimmer in the dark;
your voice bright as a sun
calls me playfully to shore.
Give me time to dry my wings,
I'll try some scales to start,
and if the music's right, a song.

2.

A glorious morning of *more!*
The hibiscus actually nodding
at the window, the slight perfume
almost a speech. It seems the world
is dense with these connections,
a throbbing of odor and touch,
light and sound, the senses keen
as Spring's velocity come down
from the Winter's north.

                    The heart
beats with the day, keeping time
that must be now, and *more*.
(which is death to hide,
and death to acknowledge,
so we live with both: the song
warming the house, and later
chilling the bone, a truth
we should long ago have known.)

3.

My stone, the Sisyphus burden,
is light as a cloud, a hoop of air,
the unending flight of thought
stretching toward despair.

It's labor without a boundary,
without time, that terrifies.
And you cry more! I hear
your exhortation of the heart,
"It's easy. Try." These bones
you ask to rise again, and sing.

4.

If days were poems, my darling,
would they might go on forever.
But poems are trails of vapor
whose great art is vanishment.
How can you call me to account
when my plan is to disappear,
a flowering of days into a mist
of days, then given to air?

A chord, an octave, mist again,
a futile reach for perfection …

5.

More poems … more love …
Is that the rush of water that drives
the wheel?
          To be a man of more
is your command. I must obey,
revise other plans, as Mozart,
ending Don Giovanni, adds
a second finale to the plot,
believed or not—
                  heavenly more!
And now, you enter, the singleness
of more, I in the wings, you
at the center.

Riddle

Don't tell me when
the ax will fall:
I'll know its weight
and call

Don't warn me when
my heart will fail:
the wind's already
in my sail

Leave me a breath
to throw a kiss:
pray to god
it won't miss

Finale

When all is said and done
and we have had our days
and watched the faithful sun
appear to rise and fall

Where voices on the air
have the only clue
along with clocks and tears
of what next to do

Days must elsewhere fly
and love to other arms
all nights converge to one
and all lovers die

RON ROLLET AND NORMAN ROSTEN
BROOKLYN HEIGHTS, NY 1987

Author's Biography

Norman Rosten, poet, playwright, novelist, was named the first Poet Laureate of Brooklyn, New York. He published seven volumes of poetry, four novels and authored several plays produced on the stage as well as on radio and television. Rosten was a longtime resident of Brooklyn and his writing often reflected his experience of growing up in Coney Island and living inBrooklyn Heights. His poems appeared in *The New Yorker, Poetry Magazine, The Atlantic Monthly, The New Republic* and many other magazines. His play, *Mister Johnson*, opened on Broadway and in London starring Earl Hyman and later James Earl Jones; Kim Hunter played Emily Dickenson in Rosten's *Come Slowly, Eden*. The music for his play *Mardi Gras* was composed by Duke Ellington. Rosten wrote the best-selling non-fiction work, *Marilyn: An Untold Story* and the libretto for Ezra Lauderman's opera, *Marilyn*, presented by the NYC Opera. Sidney Lumet directed the screenplay Rosten wrote based on his friend Arthur Miller's play, *A View From The Bridge*. Rosten received many literary awards, including those from the Yale Series of Younger Poets, the American Academy of Arts and Letters, the Poetry Society of America, as well as fellowships and grants from the Guggenheim and Ford Foundations. Rosten's wife, Hedda, authored several televised plays, and his daughter, Patricia, edited the children's book, *A City Is...*, based on his poetry.

www.ingramcontent.com/pod-product-compliance
Lightning Source LLC
Chambersburg PA
CBHW032127090426
42743CB00007B/493